# AVON SELLING SECRETS

# AVON SELLING SECRETS

sales tips from an ex-rep

T Edwards

**2nd edition**

**TE Publishing Small Press Books**
2012

ISBN-13: 978-1479192366
ISBN-10: 1479192368

*Disclaimer: This book contains information regarding general sales tactics that is the author's own opinions and experiences. It is published for general reference and is not intended to be a substitute for your own independent experiences. The publisher and author disclaim any personal or financial liability, either directly or indirectly, for the information contained within. Although the author and publisher have made every effort to ensure the accuracy and completeness of the information contained within, we assume no responsibility for errors, inaccuracies, omissions, or inconsistencies.*

*This guide is not an official guide for Avon Representatives nor is it endorsed by the Avon Company. It is merely one former Avon Representative's experiences of what worked for her, and should be approached as such.*

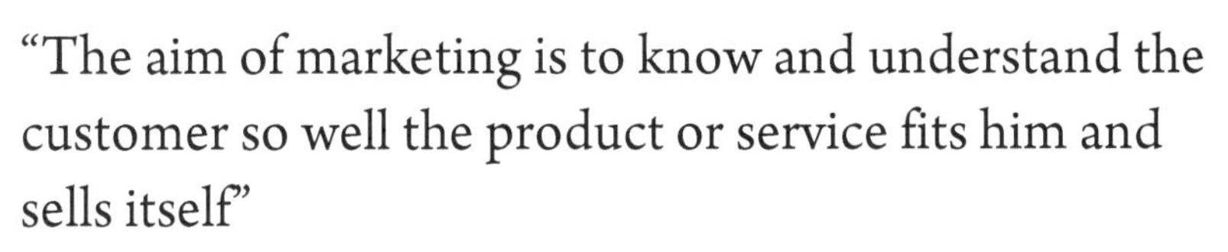

"The aim of marketing is to know and understand the customer so well the product or service fits him and sells itself"

– *Peter Drucker*

## TABLE OF CONTENTS

# ABOUT ME

Let's start with the most basic question you probably have. Who am I, and why have I written a guide for Avon Representatives?

I was, like you are now, an Avon Representative. An Avon lady if you prefer.

I decided to write this book because when I was starting out as an Avon Rep I had a lot of trouble finding customers. In fact my first order was just me and my mother. I tried tossing, I hung brochures, and did everything my upline suggested - but I was a *'shy'* Rep and didn't really want to knock on doors or talk to strangers in the streets like everyone kept telling me I should do to get sales. After a few campaigns I had a few customers, but I was nearly ready to give up because it was costing me more in brochures (*and my own purchases*) than I was making.

I knew there had to be an easier way, a way that I felt comfortable with but still made me money. So I started trying a few 'different' things that I hadn't heard anyone else trying, and that's when things started to turn around. In fact things turned around so fast I was wondering why no-one else was teaching these methods. My sales went through the roof (and so did my income), and every campaign it just grew and grew.

This guide is my experiences with what worked for me and what didn't. It contains the seven marketing techniques that helped increase my sales, step by step, including what I said, did, and gave away. It also includes the one method that helped gain me lots of customers for the least amount of effort.

I wrote it because I really hope it will help you get on the fast track to Presidents Club, Rose Circle or whatever Avon goals you might have.

Each method is set out with what you can expect in terms of customers, sales and your costs. You might have heard of the first few, but I've included them anyway with some extra tips to make them more effective because I did use them. But I'm sure you haven't heard of all of the methods. Or at least I hope you haven't, even if one of the strategies works for you it means you've made your money back.

So let's jump right in with the first method. Are you ready?

# TO TOSS OR NOT TO TOSS

## What You Can Expect

***Customers***: *Average 1 new customer for every 100 brochures you toss*
***Sales***: *Initially small orders, but they could turn into regular customers as you build trust with them.*
***Costs***: *Can be expensive due to so many brochures to purchase.*

## What is tossing?

Tossing is when you distribute your brochures to each house in an area by leaving (throwing/tossing) your brochure (usually wrapped in a *What's New* bag so it doesn't get ruined) into the yard/driveway of your potential customer.

Other variations of tossing include door hanging or leaving your brochure in the mailbox (only allowed in countries outside the USA).

This is usually the first step that many new Rep's usually take thinking that you'll get people calling you straight away to place an order.

**Is it worth it?**

While this is usually the main method taught at sales meetings, in my opinion this is not the most efficient use of your time or your money. You are giving your brochure to 'cold' customers. You have no idea if they'll be interested in your products or not, and many will not.

The strike rate for tossing is usually ***about 1 customer per 100 brochures,*** and often it takes tossing to one household up to three times to build up enough trust that people will buy from you. I have heard that some Rep's do manage to get more orders from tossing than this, but everyone I personally know has not had more than one or two customers from 100 brochures.

The only time that I recommend tossing if you have a bunch of old brochures laying around that you have no other use for, or if your upline or manager has given you a lot for free (then it won't cost you anything and is therefore worth your time). Put a label on the front with something catchy to get your customers attention.

**Some examples you could use:**

**1. Try a cute rhyme**

This brochure may be old,
But the products are still gold,
If you'd like to try a sample,
Call me, I have ample!

Examples inside of gifts galore,
Makeup, skincare, bargains and more,
The see the latest specials simply shout,
And I'll rush the latest brochure right out!

**2. The Direct approach**

Lucky you! You've got your own personal Avon Lady. She really wants you to be happy so call her for a FREE gift!

**3. Be Friendly & Casual**

Hello neighbor! I'm just up the road, if you ever run out of shower gel or need anything, just give me a call. Have a great day, [Your Name]

**4. Include a tea bag in a zip lock bag on the front of the brochure**

Have a cup of tea on me! Relax, put your feet up and browse through the brochure at your leisure. *(A fellow rep used this technique with great success by using herbal tea)*

# SIT DOWN & ENTER MY STORE

## What You Can Expect

***Customers**: Average 5 new customers for every 50 brochures left in good areas.*
***Sales**: Normal orders, usually averaging $10 - $30 per customer.*
***Costs**: Reasonable. You'll be easily able to cover brochure / gift costs with your profits.*

You've probably heard this before, but it's important to remember that your brochure is your store. Therefore your biggest challenge is to get people to open your brochure (i.e. enter your store).

The most effective way I've found to do this is to leave your brochures where people are sitting down. Coffee shops, Hairdressing salons, Launderettes, Bus or Train terminals, etc.

**Coffee Shops**

Coffee shops are particularly effective at getting new customers; people are relaxed and usually like browsing through something while they are sipping away at their lattes.

Small independent coffee shops are the best (rather than big chains like Starbucks). Go in and ask the manager if it's ok to leave a few brochures near the newspapers for the customers to browse through. Give the manager a FREE thank-you gift in return (hand soap or hand cream for their bathroom is usually a good gift — plus it has the added bonus that their customers will be using your products).

Not all coffee shops will let you leave brochures, but I've found most are fine with it as long as you ask first. Managers want their customers to hang in their shop for longer so they'll buy more coffee, that's why they provide reading material.

## Coffee Shop Challenge

***Aim*** *— To have at least FIVE Coffee Shops in your area stocking your brochures each campaign.*

***What you'll need*** *— 50 brochures, 5 to 10 FREE gifts.*

1. Go through your directory and find ten coffee shops in your area (your aim is to get your brochures into five coffee shops, but some coffee shops might say no, so make your hit list double the amount you need)

2. Ask the manager if you can leave 10 brochures next to the newspapers and in return you'll give him/her (whatever gift(s) you've chosen) as a thank-you. (Most people love something for free so they are more likely to say yes, especially if it helps their business).

3. Repeat at the next coffee shop until you've left all 50 brochures.

4. Return every campaign with new brochures.

**Expected Outcome** — From experience you usually pick up 1 to 2 customers per coffee shop each campaign. That equals 5 to 10 new customers every campaign!

**Launderettes**

A great place to find people sitting down waiting is the launderette. Leave a few brochures near any seats. However this isn't a new strategy and a lot of Reps already do this, so you might have a lot of competition - but it still doesn't hurt to leave a few anyway.

**Bus or Train terminals**

Leave a few brochures on or next to the seats where people are waiting for public transport. The best time's to do this is first thing in the morning when people are waiting to go to work.

Make sure you put them somewhere where they won't blow away because you don't want to get into trouble for littering.

**Other places**

Doctors offices, Dentists offices. While a lot of Reps already target these places it doesn't hurt to check your local medical office waiting areas to see if you might be able to leave a brochure or two.

The local HOT SPOT. This is different in every town. It's the place in your town where everyone is always at. It could be the post office, the local grocery store, or even the community hall. Whatever that place is, leave a few brochures.

# AND THE WINNER IS

## What You Can Expect

***Customers**: You'll get a lot of names and contact details.*
***Sales**: Only a few straight up, but HUGE potential for follow-up sales and even recruits.*
***Costs**: Around $50 plus a few brochures and a free gift for the salon.*

**Hairdressers/Beauty Salons**

You could do what everyone does and just leave a few brochures in the waiting room, which is fine, but if you really want to get a lot of customers in a short time then the best way to do this is to have a drawing/raffle/sweepstakes.

While it might be a big outlay to begin with, the future potential for customers definitely makes it worth your while.

Target a small to mid-size salon (one that doesn't sell cosmetics) and ask the manager if they would be interested in holding a free raffle/sweepstakes for their customers and you will supply the prize. Make sure you let the manager know what's in it for them (free entry for their customers). Because if it won't cost the manager anything, and it can boost their business, then they are usually more than happy to let you supply the prize.

Make the prize basket something enticing, I recommend spending about $50 worth of products and putting them in a pretty basket (get it from dollar stores), wrap it in clear cellophane and add a pretty ribbon. Add your business card to the basket as well. You'll also need a stack of entry forms and a box to put the entry forms into. Make the sweepstakes last no more than two weeks.

I'd also give the hairdressing salon a thank-you for letting you put the basket in the waiting area. A hand cream is great for hairdressers as they always have their hands in water and chemicals, and their hands can get quite dry.

You'll find lots of customers this way, and it's a good way to get names and contact details. This is also an excellent way to try and find potential leads to add to your team if that's what you are interested in.

An example of an entry form might look something like this (feel free to be more creative than me):

AVON SWEEPSTAKES ENTRY FORM

Name: ____________________

Address: ____________________

Phone: ____________________

Email: ____________________

☐ I'd like to receive an Avon Brochure

☐ Every two weeks ☐ Monthly ☐ Every two months

☐ Please send me more information about earning my own income

GOOD LUCK!

You don't need your contact details on the actual entry form (because the customer doesn't keep this part, you do), but it doesn't hurt to leave some business cards and some brochures in case customers want to contact you to order something as well.

Do the drawing of the winner in the salon (you could even let the manager do this). Then call and let the winner know they have won, and finally deliver the products. (*Winner's usually make excellent customers too, so make sure your business card is inside the gift basket*).

My experience of holding drawings is that you'll probably get around 100 or so entries. Of that, you will find that over half of the entrants are happy to have you send them a brochure in the future (so that's around 50+ potential customers). These are customers that you know are already interested in your products (because they entered to try and win them).

## Childcare Centres/Schools

A lot of Reps already do fundraisers at schools, so the raffle/sweepstakes could work here if there currently is no-one else doing it too, however from my experience, while you usually make a lot of money in a lump sum by doing a fundraiser at a school, the potential for continued sales is low.

There is one exception that I've found does work in getting new customers at schools, and that's coming up next.

# THERE'S NO BUSINESS LIKE SHOW BUSINESS

## What You Can Expect

***Customers:*** *Varies, but around 10-20 new customers can be expected*
***Sales:*** *Medium orders*
***Costs:*** *Your makeup to use on the actors and your time*

You've no doubt heard of other Reps giving makeovers to their customers. This follows on from that thought, and instead of giving makeovers to one, you'll be giving it to many people at once (well, sort of). What I'm talking about is to volunteer your 'services' to do the make-up at the local school play or the local amateur society. This works even better if you can round up a few other Avon Reps to help you.

*How to do this*: When you know of a play coming up in your area either at your local amateur society or school, just ring the director/teacher in charge and ask if there is anyone doing the makeup for the production and if not that you'd love to help out. Most of the times they will say that they don't have anyone doing it and are eager for you to do it for '*free*' for them.

Try and find out how many people you will need to do the makeup for so you can determine how many other Avon Reps/friends to bring along to help. As a guide you should be able to do about 4 or 5 people every thirty minutes depending on what their makeup needs are.

The best makeup to use for theatre production is the cream or mousse makeup types of foundation, blush and eye shadows. There is no need to buy any special make-up, Avon's range is perfectly suitable for stage productions. (*The exception to this is if specialized makeup is needed for certain characters eg tinman in Wizard of Oz, then the theatre production/school should supply this*)

**Some extra tips:**

- Don't bother matching foundation to skin tone exactly. Just choose a few shades darker than their normal skin tone so it gives a 'healthy' look on stage as the bright lights tend to wash out people if they have too pale a foundation.

- Use extra blush. They aren't going on a date, they are in a play.

- Black eyeliner is great for when you need to draw on 'whisker's or to color in a 'nose' to portray animals for children's productions.

- You can't notice natural eyeshadow colors on stage so feel free to use lots of color.

By now you are probably saying that this all sounds like fun and all, but how am I going to get any customers or make any money? Well there are two main ways of doing this:

**1. Program Advertising**

Ask that your name, details and phone number be included on all the programs. Something like

*MAKEUP PROVIDED BY Mary Smith, Independent Avon Representative, (555) 5555 2345*

The director/teacher in charge won't have a problem with adding something like this to the program. If you want something bigger or flashier you might have to negotiate or pay advertising, that's really up to you.

As a bonus, parents or friends of those in the play usually keep the programs for keepsakes, so your details will be with them for a long time.

**2. Sweepstakes/Drawing**

Providing a raffle/sweepstakes to everyone that attends the play is also a good idea and a great place to get customers.

Using a similar concept to the sweepstakes mentioned in the previous chapter for hair salons, everyone that buys a ticket to the show will go in the draw to win a basket full of Avon goodies and/or a free makeover or facial. Have the basket on display in the ticket area if possible and use the suggested sweepstakes tickets from the previous chapter.

# THE RECEPTIONIST IS YOUR NEW BFF

## What You Can Expect

***Customers***: *Around 20 new customers per 30 offices visited (avg 6 offices will order with 3-4 girls from each).*
***Sales***: *Higher orders (these girls have disposable income!).*
***Costs***: *You'll be easily able to cover brochure / samples costs with your profits.*

***** This method is my favorite way to gain customers (and profits) quickly *****

You already know that I'm a fan of customers that are sitting down. And what better place to have a lot of customers in the same area, (all with disposable incomes), than those that sit at desks in the workplace.

One of the quickest ways that I increased my sales was to target other businesses, in particular office buildings. What I would do is to go into an office building and say to the receptionist something like '*Hi, I'm giving out free samples to all the girls in your office today, how many girls work here?*' She'd reply that fifteen girls worked there, so I'd say '*Great, here are your samples*' and put about fifteen lipstick samples and fifteen skincare samples (or whatever I was promoting that campaign) on her desk along with three or four brochures (**with order forms inside them of course**).

I'd tell her I was coming back in three days for the brochures as I recycled them (I would do my drops on a Monday and pick up on a Thursday). Then I'd simply say goodbye and thank her and leave. The important thing here is for her to think that you are simply giving out free gifts, not pushing for orders. Then she'll likely go and give all the girls in the office their 'freebies'.

When I came back on the Thursday I'd say, *'Hi I'm here to pick up the brochures I left on Monday'*. Never ask if there are any orders, just smile and pick up your brochures.

More often than not, I'd find that the receptionist would say as soon as I walked in, *'Oh Suzie from Accounts loved that moisturizer! Here is her order'* or something along those lines. And if one person orders from the office it creates a snowball effect and lots of people from that same office will start ordering. Especially if you **deliver their products to the office**, then everyone will see what they got and want some too.

This is a very effective way of getting brochures out there with low overheads (samples are usually more cost effective than brochures).

The office buildings in my area were typically 15-20 stories high with around 3 to 4 businesses on each level. If you do the math that's around 50 businesses per building and with at least 10 girls in each office, that's at least 500 potential customers in the one building.

## Office Building Challenge

***Aim*** *— Target one new office building every campaign.*

***What you'll need*** *— Start with around 200 samples and approximately 50 brochures, or whatever you can afford to start with. A few inexpensive gifts (only give to the receptionist if there are orders).*

1. Choose the office building you are going to start with. Have a look at the directory on the ground floor to get an idea of how many floors the building has, and how many businesses are on each level.

2. Ignore any 'No hawking/soliciting signs'. (I never had any problems, but if you do, just apologize and go to the next business/building)

3. Start with the first floor. Go to the receptionist and tell her you are giving out free samples to the girls in her office, and ask her how many girls work there. Give her two different samples per girl (i.e. if there are 10 girls that work there, give the receptionist 10 lipstick and 10 skincare samples), and leave a few brochures. I used to leave 1 brochure for every 5 girls that worked there, so 10 girls equals 2 brochures.

4. The reason for only leaving a few brochures is that it creates demand, if one girl sees another reading the brochure they'll want to have a look, but if everyone has one then the excitement is lost. However if the receptionist does ask for more brochures, then of course give them to her.

5. Smile and tell the receptionist that you'll be back on (whatever day you plan to return) to recycle the brochures. Say thank-you and leave.

6. Write down how many brochures and samples you gave out to that office.

7. Repeat with the next office until you either run out of brochures, samples, or run out of time.

8. Return in a few days to pick up the brochures (and hopefully some orders!) ***Important*** - Don't ask if there were any orders unless the receptionist offers, just say thank-you and take your brochures.

9. If there were any orders, let them know when you will be back and how much each person owes. Give the receptionist a small gift (lip balm or hand cream) as a thank you (*only give the receptionist a gift if there are orders. It's not a bribe, it's a thank you*).

10. Return to each office every campaign for three campaigns (if they don't order by then, it's time to move on to a new office)

**Expected Outcome** — This technique EXPLODED my sales. As an added bonus it's very cost and time effective.

Nearly every office I went into accepted the samples (everyone loves a freebie). The first time I did this I visited about 30 businesses and 6 of them ordered. From the 6 that did place orders, each had around 3 to 4 girls from that office that placed orders so that was 20 new customers from one campaign. And the orders from offices are often higher than household orders too.

# FLYER WAY WITH ME

## What You Can Expect

***Customers***: *1 to 2 new customers for every 5 flyers you put up*
***Sales***: *Initially small orders, but they could turn into regular customers as you build trust with them.*
***Costs***: *CHEAP! Just paper.*

Are you creative? Making a Flyer can be a cost effective way to find new customers because you will only be paying for the paper and the copying (depending on how many you print up).

I've found that the return rate isn't brilliant; you might only get one or two new customers from every 5 or so Flyers per campaign, but while you won't have a huge rush of customers beating down your door, I still think it's worthwhile due to the low overheads to produce.

The two most important things to include on your Flyer is

1) a way for the customer to take your details away with them (either pull off tabs at the bottom of the Flyer, or attaching business cards to the Flyer) and

2) you've got to make it eye-catching to get your customers attention in the first place.

**How to make your Flyer eye-catching**

1. **Color** — This is, of course, a no-brainer, but colored Flyers get noticed almost five times more than black and white ones. You can achieve color in two ways: either using colored paper, OR white paper with colored pictures and text. Whichever you decide will depend on your resources. Some of you may have a color printer at home; others may only have a black & white printer. If you choose the colored paper option, use really bright colors to catch attention, but make sure that you can still read the text that is on it.

A good trick is to use the colored paper as a border and add the white paper with your message on it in the middle (as I've demonstrated in the example on the next page)

2. **Picture** — A picture is great, but keep it simple. Try to keep it to one or two that fit the theme of the flyer. That way the customer can focus on the message and the call to action.

3. **Think of a cute attention grabbing title** — Keep the title to five words or less. This guarantee's that the customers will be able to read it quickly as she's scanning the flyer. Most people scan before they read. You need to get her attention in three seconds or less and fewer words work best.

4. **Use the word FREE somewhere on the flyer** — Nothing creates more action than the magic word FREE. People will contact you for the freebie (a low cost item to you like a sample)

5. **One message per flyer** — Think about the large companies advertisements. It's always only ONE message per billboard/magazine ad. You don't want to overload with information. If you have more than one message to get out, then simply create more than one flyer.

**Contact Details**

You could leave your details on how to order/contact you via three methods:

1. **On the bottom of the flyer** — While this is important (in case all the pull-tabs/business cards are removed), it should not be your only method of leaving your details. Most customers aren't going to go to the bother of writing down your details and then calling you. Make it easy for them by leaving something for them to take away.

2. **Pull-tabs** — Have your details on pieces of paper stuck to the flyer. The easiest way to do this is to cut slits in the bottom of the flyer with your details so the customer can tear off your details and take it with them.

3. **Business Cards** — Attached to the side of the flyer. Business Cards are my preference since they are study and can hold a lot of information. Sometimes pull-tabs can get torn and are more easily damaged, but business cards tend to get kept more often.

Here is an example of a flyer using all my tips:

Choose a simple but attention grabbing title
Attach your business cards so customers can grab your details and take it with them
Psst! KISS & TELL
Want to know how to get plump sexy lips for less ?
Avon lipsticks now only $2.99
Call me for your FREE sample
Jane Smith, Avon Rep, 555 1
email@address.com
Jane Smith
Avon Rep
555 1234
email@address.com
Use colored paper behind to create a border to attract attention

# HERE COMES THE BRIDE

## What You Can Expect

***Customers**: Lots of friends wanting to spend money on the Bride-To-Be. Some people will go on to become regular customers.*
***Sales**: Once off orders of at least $100 ++ per party, and if you have a table at a bridal show you'll probably book at least 10 brides (if not more!), so your sales will be very high.*
***Costs**: Booking a table at a Bridal show, your time and some demonstration products.*

Do you know of anyone getting married? Guess what, brides love to spend money on things that are going to make them beautiful for their big day. And here is your chance to show that how beautiful they can be with Avon products.

There are numerous ways of making money with weddings, such as offering bridal makeup, however the most effective way of increasing your sales is to host a bridal shower or hen/doe night.

The easiest way to find potential brides is to set up a table at your local bridal expo or bridal show. Make the table as pretty and fun looking as you can. White tulle makes a great tablecloth and sprinkling confetti around makes it seem festive and fun. Have a big sign with ideas of fun bridal showers that you can do. Try and be creative and think about some fun party games or themes that you could offer such as:

**Pillow Pamper Party** — *Everyone gets to be pampered and relax from the stresses of life while sampling beautiful makeup and fragrances from Avon.*

**Cinderella Foot Spa** — *Soak your cares away while being pampered at this fun and relaxing foot spa.*

***Bridesmaids Revenge*** — *Maids it's your chance to makeover the bride at this fun party guaranteed to make you laugh and have a great time. (This is one is always popular for me)*

Whatever theme you choose, cater the demonstration products to that theme. For example, at a foot spa, you'll need something to soak everyone's feet in (cheap buckets can be bought at dollar stores). Have some towels on hand and of course the products you are going to use, such as Skin So Soft bath oil (for soaking feet), nail polish and polish remover, body scrub for the feet and legs and body moisturizer etc.

The biggest way to have a successful party is to have some music playing, good food and good wine (supplied by the host). Your job is to make it FUN FUN FUN FUN! So try not to be too 'sales'y. By all means have some brochures and some order forms there but don't stand up and say a spiel on every product. The orders will come easier if you make each guest (and especially the bride) feel like it's about THEM and not YOU.

As a thank-you to the bride you can:

1. Give a gift basket made up with pampering products. Put them in a nice basket and theme it bridal by popping in a garter or something bride'ish. Tie with cellophane and a white ribbon; OR

2. Have an empty basket full of envelopes. During the course of the party, guests can make a 'donation' in an envelope. At the end of the party the bride can spend all the envelope money on products that she wants.

If you are booking from a bridal show make sure you have your diary with you because you will get bookings. For every booking, give the bride or maid (whoever books you) a little thank-you bag with some samples inside. From experience, the best day to hold the parties are on Saturday afternoons because everyone is in a relaxed frame of mind, however consider your own schedule first to see what suits you the best.

# FAST TRACK TO SUCCESS

I've included a quick plan built over five campaigns to help you fast track your way to success. You may follow the plan I've suggested or write your own plan based on your own personal goals. The next chapter will help you set goals of your own to help you reach your Avon dreams.

## First Campaign

***Order: 150 brochures, 3 hand creams, 30 lipstick samples, 30 skincare or fragrance samples***

- Drop 10 brochures each at 3 coffee shops in your area (give hand creams to managers as thank-you's).
- Visit 5-6 businesses (or however many it takes to give out 30 samples).
- Leave 10 brochures at your local HOT SPOT
- Leave 10 brochures at either a Laundromat or Medical waiting room
- Make up 3 flyers to place on bulletin boards in your area.
- Toss approx 50 brochures (I know you are going to try this anyway so I might as well include it here)
- Keep the remainder of brochures for your current customers and friends.

## Second Campaign

***Order: 200 brochures, 3 hand creams, 60 lipstick samples, 60 skincare or fragrance samples***

- Drop 10 brochures each at the current 3 coffee shops you did last campaign and find 3 new coffee shops this campaign (give hand creams to managers at new coffee shops as thank-you's).
- Visit 10-12 businesses, include the offices that you visited previously and visit some new ones. (however many it takes to give out 60 samples).
- Leave 10 new brochures at your local HOT SPOT
- Make up 3 new flyers to place on bulletin boards in your area.
- Find out if any schools or amateur groups are holding a show in the next few months.
- Toss approx 75 brochures
- Keep the remainder of brochures for your current customers and friends.

## Third Campaign

***Order: 250 brochures, 4 hand creams, 100 lipstick samples, 100 skincare or fragrance samples***

- Drop 10 brochures each at the current 6 coffee shops you did last campaign and find 4 new coffee shops this campaign (give hand creams to managers at new coffee shops as thank-you's). Now you will have a base of 10 coffee shops stocking your brochures.
  - Visit businesses, including the offices that you visited previously and visit some new ones. (However many it takes to give out 100 samples).
- Leave 10 new brochures at your local HOT SPOT
- Make up 5 new flyers to place on bulletin boards in your area.
- Inquire about bridal shows/expos in your area. Think about what sort of fun party you would be interested in showing.
- Toss approx 100 brochures
- Keep the remainder of brochures for your current customers and friends.

## Fourth Campaign

***Order: 300 brochures, 100 lipstick samples, 100 skincare or fragrance samples, $50 worth of product for a gift basket sweepstakes***

- Drop 10 brochures each at your coffee shops.
- Visit businesses, stop going to any business that haven't ordered from you yet (if they haven't ordered after three times, move on), visit your regular offices and find new ones. (However many it takes to give out 100 samples).
- Leave 10 new brochures at your local HOT SPOT
- Make up 5 new flyers to place on bulletin boards in your area.
- Approach a hair/beauty salon about holding a sweepstakes to win a hamper full of Avon products.
- Toss approx 100 brochures
- Keep the remainder of brochures for your current customers and friends.

## Fifth Campaign

***Order: 300 brochures (or however many you need as you will have a good idea now of how many to order), 100 lipstick samples, 100 skincare or fragrance samples, $50 worth of product for a gift basket sweepstakes***

- Drop 10 brochures each at your coffee shops.
- Visit businesses, dump any business that hasn't ordered from you after three times, visit your regular offices and find new ones. (However many it takes to give out 100 samples).
- Leave 10 new brochures at your local HOT SPOT
- Make up 5 new flyers to place on bulletin boards in your area.
- Do the drawing from your previous sweepstakes and drop brochures to customers that indicated on their sweepstakes form that they wanted to see a brochure.
- Approach another hair/beauty salon in a different area about holding a sweepstakes to win a hamper full of Avon products.
- Toss approx 100 brochures

- Keep the remainder of brochures for your current customers and friends.

## Sixth and further Campaign's

By now you should be so busy with LOTS of customers, LOTS of orders and LOTS of profit for you. Just keep doing what you are doing and let the business grow to a level you are comfortable with.

# SETTING GOALS

Sometimes trying to achieve your dreams can seem like an enormous task, but I actually find that putting things down onto paper and working out the steps logically can make things seem much more attainable. There is an old saying that I think is just wonderful: "The only difference between dreams and goals is that goals have a timeline". It makes anything seem possible if you have a schedule for it.

## *Goal example*: Make $500 profit every campaign

Say for example that your goal was to make a profit of $500 per campaign. It might sound a lot, but I think it's definitely doable (after all there are lots of other Avon Reps making much more than this so there is no reason that you can't as well).

At a 40% commission rate that means that you will have to sell approximately $1,300 worth of Avon (probably slight more to take into account your costs). If the average customer spends $30, that means you are going to need around 43 or 44 customers ($1,300 / $30 = 43.3).

**What do you need to do to find 44 customers?**

You could try tossing. Although with the strike rate of 1 customer for every 100 brochures, that would mean you'd need 4,400 brochures! YIKES — who has the time for that!

I suggest using one or more of the methods outlined in this guide. For example, you could get 6 or 7 customers from dropping at coffee shops, 20 or more customers from businesses, 10-20 from doing a sweepstake/raffle, and an extra 1 or 2 from flyers that you place around. That's around 44 new customers (and much less work than tossing over 4,000 brochures!)

Now it's your turn. What are your goals?

# PROFIT YOU'D LIKE

$ ______________________________________________

What sales level do you need to reach to achieve this goal?

$ ______________________________________________

Assuming an average order of $30, how many customers do you need to reach that sales level?

$ ______________________________________________

What steps can you do to increase your customer base to that level?

1. ______________________________________________

2. ______________________________________________

3. ______________________________________________

4. ______________________________________________

5. ______________________________________________

# BONUS SALES TIPS

On the following pages are some of the articles and blog posts that I've published over the years with some extra sales tips for you.

Included articles:

*Where Do You Find Avon Customers?*
*Finding More Avon Customers & Increasing Your Sales*
*Avon Christmas Selling Tips*
*Valentine's Day Selling Tips*

## Where Do You Find Avon Customers?

As a new Representative (*or an existing Rep looking to increase your business*), you are probably wondering where to find your customers.

Here is a quick list of some of my favorite places for finding new Avon customers.

**#1. Friends/Family**

Ok, so you already know this one, but friends and family truly are the best places to start. Sometimes family members can be a bit skeptical at first, but if you act positive usually they'll respond positively back.

Often I've found a good tactic for a friend or family member who says *'You'll never make money with Avon'* is to reply,*'Maybe you could help me get started then, can you leave a few brochures at your work/playgroup/hangout for me?'*. Usually you'll get a reluctant yes, but then a few days later they'll be so proud of themselves for getting you a few orders.

**#2. Tossing/Dropping Brochures**

I'm sure we have all done this one with varying degrees of success, and while this isn't my preferred method of finding customers, if you are consistent you can build up a good customer base.

Usually it takes between 3 to 5 times before someone will order from you, and as a general rule for every 100 brochures you put out, you might receive only 1 or 2 orders.

In the beginning this method will probably only have you break even with your costs, but if you remain consistent and toss every single campaign *(or until a customer says they don't wish to see a brochure anymore)* then you can build up to about 25-30 per 100 houses over at least 7-10 campaigns.

After a house hasn't ordered after 10 campaigns then it's up to you whether to continue to drop at that house or not. I usually leave it for a while, but then drop again at Christmas.

If you decide not to continue dropping at that house, sometimes it's nice to include a little note after the 10th campaign that says something like:

"HI, I'M [YOUR NAME], YOUR LOCAL AVON REPRESENTATIVE, I HOPE YOU'VE ENJOYED SEEING ALL THE LOVELY ITEMS AVON HAS IN THE BROCHURES, IF YOU'D LIKE TO CONTINUE TO SEE THEM EACH CAMPAIGN (OR LESS OFTEN IF YOU PREFER), THEN GIVE ME A QUICK CALL/EMAIL AND I'LL MAKE SURE YOU REMAIN ON MY LIST OF HOUSES TO DROP TO."

Keeping it friendly and no pressure usually works best.

**#3. Talking to people you meet**

When you meet new people and they ask you what you do, what do you say? Instead of just replying "I do Avon" or "I sell Avon", I find the best opening line is to say something enticing and interesting like "I LET PEOPLE PAMPER THEMSELVES AT HOME USING AVON PRODUCTS" or the less pushy "I LET PEOPLE ORDER THEIR AVON THROUGH ME DIRECT FROM THE COMPANY".

Saying something different like this usually starts a conversation and then you can ask if they've seen a brochure recently and build from there.

**#4. Talking to Strangers**

One of the hardest things to do for most new reps (and even experienced reps!) is to ask a stranger if they are interested in Avon.

I find the best way is to either be casually browsing a brochure yourself and if anyone seems to be paying attention to what you are doing, smile and say 'have you seen the latest brochure?'.

A fellow rep had great success with carrying around a hand cream in her purse. At any sitting opportunity (bus, coffee shop, and picking up kids from school) she would apply the hand cream and ask if anyone else needed to use some. Very often people would say yes and then comment on how lovely the hand cream was, at which she would apply, 'OH I'M AN AVON REP, IF YOU EVER NEED ANY YOURSELF I CAN GET IT FOR YOU..'

Clever huh!

# Finding More Avon Customers & Increasing Your Sales.

The main difference between a successful Avon Representative and one that is struggling is the amount of customers that they have. Find more customers and invariably you'll increase your sales. That's all well and good, but once you've gone through all your family and friends, how DO you find more people that want to buy Avon? Here are some of my favorite tips for increasing your customer base.

You've all heard the tips for standing in parking lots or shopping centres to hand out brochures right? Well I don't know about you but I hate going up to perfect strangers and introducing myself. Sure you can say "HI, I'M CINDY AN AVON REPRESENTATIVE, WOULD YOU LIKE A BROCHURE?', and I'm sure it would work SOMETIMES - but I don't know about you, but I HATE JUST APPROACHING PEOPLE I DON'T KNOW TRYING TO GET NEW BUSINESS.

So instead you need to **think smarter about your Avon business**.

The two main areas you'll need to concentrate on are **marketing** and **advertising**, just like a regular business.

Getting business cards is a good idea. Print them yourself on your home printer if you want to do it for free.

You can make flyers, brochures, postcards or just use the Avon brochure with your Avon selling strategy.

**Think About WHO Your Customer Is**

Put your business thinking cap on - what type of customers are interested in buying avon products? Stay at home moms who can't get to the shops easily, older couples who aren't so mobile any more, regular busy working women?

Now think about where they hang out: Moms - at home, Working Women - offices, Elderly Women - home or retirement village.

Your next step is to CREATE A MARKETING STRATEGY AROUND YOUR SPECIFIC CUSTOMER.

**LET'S USE THE STAY AT HOME MOM AS AN EXAMPLE.**

She doesn't have a lot of time (who does these days!) so make things easy for her to buy from you. Create a Mom Pamper Pack!

In the pack include a brochure, your business card, a few samples, and order form and an envelope. Put it in a nice little bag (SEE THROUGH ONES ARE BEST - I'VE FOUND USING FREEZER BAGS FROM THE GROCERY STORE ARE GREAT AND VERY ECONOMICAL).

Put a nice message or note attached to the front of the bag or brochure. Something like: "I THOUGHT YOU WOULD ENJOY SOME TIME OUT FOR YOURSELF, ENJOY THE SAMPLES AND IF YOU EVER NEED TO ORDER ANYTHING JUST PUT THE ORDER FORM IN THE ENVELOPE AND I'LL BE AROUND AT FRIDAY 10A.M. TO COLLECT IT, TAKE CARE AND HAVE A GREAT DAY, CINDY".

Hang the brochure on her door knob or leave at the front step.

It's friendly - non threatening and likely to get a good response. I'd continue doing it every few weeks until either she orders or tells you that she isn't interested in buying Avon.

## Christmas Selling Ideas

There is something about the holiday season that brings out the shopper in all of us. All in all, the holidays are a pretty magical time. Or are they? In reality it's more likely that we've got to clean up the house in time for visitors, tackle the crowds at the mall, and make sure that everyone is entertained.

So as an Avon Representative, this Christmas it's your job to make things less stressful for your customers and your reward will be lovely big orders and plenty of profits for you.

**Tip 1: Send your customers cards to make them feel special**

Start by sending your customers a Christmas or Holiday card. The earlier that you can get this card out the better - late October/early November is ideal. This makes them feel special, that you are thinking of them during this busy time.

**Tip 2: Give them a holiday gift planner**

When you next visit your customers, add little extra's to help them organize their lives such as a gift idea's list. A holiday calendar planner is also a great addition to help your customers, especially if you add a magnet to the back so that they can place it on the fridge.

**Tip 3: Offer Free Gift Wrapping**

Offer gift wrapping for free. You can pick up nice paper at dollar stores or use clear cellophane with a pretty bow. Extra touches like these can increase customer orders and create loyalty.

**Tip 4: Make Gift Baskets**

For those customers that can't decide, why not offer to make a gift basket for them. They can choose the amount they'd like to spend and a theme, such as bath & body, or feet treats, and you can fill the basket with lovely goodies that you think would love.

Gift baskets are also a great idea for your male customers. They usually don't know what to buy the ladies in their lives and offering a gift basket all wrapped and decorated for them makes things easy for them, and their partner will love it.

### Tip 5: Give Them Gifts

Want to reward your best customers? Make your customers feel special by giving them a free gift with their orders to say thank you for being a great customer. Choose something that costs you little but has a high perceived value and your customers will be thrilled. It doesn't have to be anything expensive, a hand cream or lip balm is perfect. Little touches like these can help build your business and gain lots of repeat customers because you are going that extra mile for them.

### Tip 6: Give Out More Brochures at Christmas Time

Give a brochure to everyone you know (including those that haven't previously purchased from you). Friends, family, neighbors all need to buy gifts for their loved ones so make it easy for them. If you are worried about appearing pushy then say it in a really casual tone, "Here's the latest brochure, if you want anything just give me a call" and leave it at that.

Tossing can be lucrative this time of year with everyone wanting gift ideas Some people like to roll and toss (roll up the brochure and secure with a rubber band), however try using a cute Christmassy ribbon instead to grab attention. Even better is to hang your brochure on the front door knob of your customer's houses so they will see their 'gift' when they arrive home.

### Tip 7: Give Out Christmas Decorations

Use lipstick samples as Christmas tree decorations! Just add some sparkly string to tie to the tree, or put them in little clear bags and hang the bags. These are also great to give out to potential customers, just make sure you include your business card as well!

## Valentine Days Sales Tips

Valentine's Day is actually a great way to increase your customer base and improve on your Avon sales, especially with men who often are clueless about what to get their partner as a gift. Here are some of my favorite tips and gift basket ideas for the romantic in all of us.

**Dust off those poetry skills.**

Why not add a poem to the front of your Avon brochures?

*"Roses are Red, Lipstick is too.*
*Your secret admirer can buy from me too.*
*Have a quick look and circle your choice,*
*Hand it to HIM so he can rejoice."*

**How to Display your Avon Brochures**

Often around holiday selling times I like to add special treats to my brochure bags to entice customers to buy. Valentine's Day works best if you add a candy to 'sweeten' your customer up. But don't use chocolate - it can melt and create a huge mess. The best candy to use (if you can find them) are those old fashioned candy hearts with writing on them. If you can't find them, any heart shaped candy will work.

**Gift Basket Ideas**

Men always need ideas on what to get their loved ones for Valentine's Day so make things easy on them - offer readymade gift baskets in certain themes.

Here are my favorite themed gift baskets for Valentine's Day (make sure you price them well too):

***Feet Treat Basket***

Fill a basket with Avon Footworks products, a nail brush and a face washer. Add a 'certificate' from the gift giver for a FREE foot massage.

***So Sexy & Sensual Bath Delights Basket***

(A play on the SSS of the Avon Skin So Soft name). Fill your basket with a few SSS products, a scented candle and a CD of romantic music. All she has to do is have a bath and enjoy a fun evening *(*wink*)*.

***Red Hot Mama Basket***

A bottle of perfume (The Avon Christian Lacroix 'Rouge' perfume works well because of the sexy red bottle), a bright red Avon lipstick and some shimmer powder. Add red tissue paper to the gift basket. *(You can add more items to this gift basket depending on what price you want to make it, but make sure they are colored RED).*

I'm sure you can come up with many more creative ideas as well!

# OTHER TOOLS YOU MIGHT NEED

**Business Cards**

While business cards are not essential, I think they give you more credibility as a business person. Don't bother getting the special ones through Avon that includes a logo, they are too expensive. I prefer to get mine free through VistaPrint. Choose a design that suits your business and that's it, you only have to pay for postage. Don't forget to add your title — Avon Independent Sales Representative so people know what you do!

An alternative is to design and print them yourself if you have a printer at home. You can get business card paper templates at your local stationery store.

**Address Labels**

I also get my address labels from VistaPrint when they are offered free. Then I just stick my contact details on the back of brochures and I'm good to go.

However it's also very easy to print your own (if you have a printer).

**Car Decal/Sign**

Definitely worth it. It's only a onetime cost and then it's free advertising as you drive around your town.

A lot of reps also have lots of luck with a brochure hanger attached to the window that they leave brochures in while they are off shopping. I personally tried this and while a lot of brochures were taken, no-one followed up with any orders so it's up to you whether you try this technique.

Well that's all of my best tips that have worked well for me and I believe will work well for you too. If you have any success stories from any of my techniques I'd love to hear them.

I wish you all the best for your success as an Avon Representative.

# INDEX

Made in the USA
Lexington, KY
19 June 2013